You are the Most Essential Brand

Witson Anyatonwu

You are the Most Essential Brand

Copyright © 2017 Witson Anyatonwu

Email: youarethemostessentialbrand@gmail.com

All rights reserved. No part of this book may be reproduced or transmitted in any form or by any means, electronic or mechanical, including photocopying, recording, or by any information storage and retrieval system, without permission in writing from the author.

ISBN: 97850300210
ISBN-13: 978-978-50302-1-1

Published by Chiysonovelty International

Printed in the United States of America

Foreword

You are ordinary! You are the most beautiful and the very best; you have being called to unending success. You are excellent in every single aspect of your life. Nothing is too good for you, or beyond your reach. You have what it takes to influence the system that drives the progress of humanity.

In this mind-blowing and ground-breaking masterpiece, YOU ARE THE MOST ESSENTIAL BRAND, the author Witson Anyatonwu has given you unique elements of purposeful and successful living that will empower you to shine your light and improve your world.

You are the most essential brand the world is waiting for! You are the one to change your world and your country. The wisdom and freedom, the beauty and integrity, the sapience and excellence, the boldness and goodness you will ever need to make new discoveries and proffer new thoughts and ideas that will empower you step out from the crowd and crown yourself with success are wrapped up in this life-changing book.

Refuse to let your mind go to sleep. Read this work of genius and break new grounds, blaze new trails and chart new frontiers. There is no better time to go out of your depth and do things that are beyond your depth than in this day and age. This is the best time to impact the world with the investment of your influence...I recommend to you, YOU ARE THE MOST ESSENTIAL BRAND.

Anyaele Sam Chiyson

President/CEO–Chiysonovelty Int'l.

CONTENTS

	Dedication	VIII
	Introduction	Pg #1
1	Set a Goal . Take Action	Pg #6
2	Be Optimistic	Pg #13
3	Focus	Pg #18
4	Compassion	Pg #23
5	Attitude	Pg #27
6	Confidence	Pg #32
7	Creativity	Pg #37
8	Purpose	Pg #42
9	Commitment	Pg #48
10	Strength/Weakness	Pg #53
11	Health	Pg #59
12	Self Control/Will Power	Pg #63
13	Balance	Pg #68
14	Financial Freedom	Pg #75
15	Giving	Pg #84

This is a very useful, nay, essential book for anyone desirous of achieving success in life. The contents of this book are dynamite for self-improvement and purposeful living. The size of the book may be misleading because the contents are life-changing. I read this book with great interest and when I was done with the first read, I had no choice but to re-read the book. Believe me, the author has done his readers a great favour.

The book boils down in readable and attractive style, the nuggets of hard truths which if followed are definitely bound to rewire the mind of anyone seriously desirous of making something important out of an otherwise dull and shambolic life.

The fifteen key elements of purposeful and successful living are broken down to granular details. This book is a must-read and I recommend it to any serious-minded person.

Prof. Ikechi Mgbeoji

Osgoode Hall Law School, Toronto

You Are The Most Essential Brand is a fabulous and fantastic piece of intellectual product.

Macnoble Emeka Akawason

Teacher, English Language and Literature, College Of Science & Knowledge Studies Beylikduzu Istanbul Turkey

DEDICATION

To Ugom and My Wonderful Family.

INTRODUCTION

Do you ever wonder why migration is always from less developed areas to more and most developed areas? Have you seen or heard about birds picking sands in the stead of grains? Even a goat, in its presumed low IQ will always choose greener pastures! Do you know why? Packaging, then CONTENT matters a lot when it comes to products and services.

Most times, people grumble about lack of jobs. However, are there actually no jobs? For me, the bitter truth is; if there is lack of anything per se, it is lack of expertise! There are not enough skills. The world is constantly changing and if a person does not change with it, the world will continue without them.

Now the question is are we prepared to change with the tide? Are we ready to embrace the FUTURE? Are we willing to be positive to face realities of the oncoming change without FEAR, BITTERNESS, and or ANGER towards anything or anyone?

CHANGE is a norm… but how many of us realize this?

You cannot be successful if you constantly try to become what everyone else is! To be successful, you do not need to fit in rather you must stand out! You are unique, so is everyone.

The focus of *YOU ARE THE MOST*

ESSENTIAL BRAND is on personal development. Its aim is to improve your character (*content*). You CANNOT give what you do not have; hence, there is need for you to improve as often as you can.

Destiny they say is our character and of a truth, we can effect or affect.

Your composure – the way you appear, speak, or even think, matters a lot. Be it physically or online. Your circles of friends also make or mar you.

If you want to be great, think great.

The size of your thoughts, its purity, and your ability to remember your true self will definitely get you into the gathering of likeminded people. If you want to be a musician, think like one, visit music studios, and not a stadium, listen, and watch musicals and not football games.

The truth is that we are what we think, and our environment influences us. *YOU ARE THE MOST ESSENTIAL BRAND* will help you reshape your character (*destiny*) towards making your path to understanding your true self a reality. A friend of mine lost his job at a multinational firm but before he got his termination letter, three other multinationals were up for his signature even with better offers. When I was working with one Pension Fund Administrator (*PFA*), I could remember vividly other PFAs were chasing my Regional Manager's signature as if no one else could do it better.

On similar occasions, I have seen a situation in which firms flew in technicians from other cities to do a job in a locality where technicians abound. It is all about being exceptional in whatever you do. Do not just be *"an akaraseller"*, be *"theakaraseller"* and people will look for you and what you can offer.

What am I saying? When you really invest in yourself, you sure will reap bountifully. Remember packaging, then content! This book will reposition you for prosperity and success in your chosen career.

Buckle up and let us ride…

CHAPTER ONE

SET A GOAL. TAKE ACTION

"What you do, not what you say you will do is all it takes to make a difference in life"
– Witson Anyatonwu.

Deciding what you want in life is arguably the most difficult and certainly the most important and rewarding thing to do. It is very vital to self-development. You have to be careful when it comes to considering what you want in order to achieve success. Goal setting entails separating what is important from what is irrelevant. Goal setting in other words is simply "*Action Plan*".

Bringing dreams from realms of imagination to reality needs a clear-cut plan. You have to be precise. Write them down. A goal written down is on its way to reality. The big corporations, innovations and many others all began with dreams, imaginations, and most importantly the "will" to start.

Let us discuss about goals, for it is only when we understand it that we could properly set attainable goals.

A goal, simply put is the object of your ambition, intent, plan, design, or desired result. A good goal is time-bound and of measurable and observable end result.

Many people world over feel adrift. They work so hard in their chosen careers but they do not seem to get anywhere worthwhile. Do you know why? It is because they have not spent enough time to plan, to design and define their ambitions. No one set out on a journey with no real intent.

Goal setting is a process of deciding about an ideal future, and motivating yourself towards turning your vision(s) to reality. This process helps to direct you in the right path. By knowing what you want to achieve precisely, you would know where you have to channel your efforts and at the same time, you will be able to spot and avoid distractions.

WHY SET A GOAL?

Achievers in all fields, be it business, sports, technology, etc. set goals. Setting goals gives you a broad vision and strong motivation; it helps you stay true on your lane. When you set a goal, long or short term you will discover it helps you to organise your time and resources.

By setting a *'SMART'* goal, you have raised your self-confidence and competency towards achieving it.

HOW TO SET A SMART GOAL:

The best way of making goals more powerful is to use the SMART mnemonic.

SMART could stand for:

S - Significant (*Specific*)

M - Meaningful (*Measurable*)

A - Action – oriented (*Attainable*)

R - Rewarding (*Relevant*)

T - Track-able (*Time-bound*)

Given the meaning of SMART, you can set effective and achievable goals.

Take for instance, instead of "TO BUILD A WORLD CLASS LIBRARY" as a goal; it is more powerful to use the SMART goal "TO HAVE BUILT A WORLD CLASS LIBRARY BY DECEMBER 2017".

The later will obviously be attainable if we put preparations in place before hand. When setting a goal, express and state each goal with high level of positivity. Be precise. Set dates, time, and amounts. These techniques will help you execute and achieve your chosen goal(s).

If you have several goals, list them in order of priority. This will help you avoid being overwhelmed and will direct your attention towards achieving the most important ones first.

KEY POINTS:

Goal setting is an important method of:

- Taking decisions, absolute responsibility of one's life.
- Separating relevant from irrelevant things.
- Motivating oneself and building self-confidence upon successful achievements.

It is advisable to set your lifetime goals

first. Then a five year plan of lesser goals that you need to achieve, if you must meet your lifetime target. You have to always review and update your goals.

Lastly, do not forget to reward yourself appropriately each time you achieve a goal. It helps build your self-confidence.

CHAPTER TWO

BE OPTIMISTIC

"Those who wish to sing, always find a song." – Swedish parable.

Being optimistic is a mental attitude. It is a disposition or tendency of looking on the brighter side of any condition and of expecting the most favourable outcome of such a condition. It does not matter what other people think about you, what matters is what you think of yourself.

Donald J. Trump, before he became the president of the United States of America was a businessperson. Nobody gave him a chance but he rose to power against all odds. The mainstream media all over the world, the political class, even his own party (*The Republicans*) stood between him and his goal of becoming the POTUS. In spite of his challenges, he did not deter. In his words, *"my whole life is all about winning I don't lose often. I almost never lost"*. He fought with brutality, with every available weapon in his arsenal. He was tough. His thought was so big. He was precise and focused knowing that people will measure him not by how much he undertook but by what he could achieve in the end.

Before Barack Obama became the POTUS, one could bet he would never be. Owing to the seemingly high odds against him (*He is black, of African root and he was not the popular choice according to pundits*). Nevertheless, he did not allow people to dictate for him. He believed in himself and he accomplished his goal of becoming the first black man in-charge of America!

What is it that you have in mind to achieve? What is the size of your dream(s)? It takes conviction, confidence, and belief to achieve dreams.

Our minds are like personal computers. What you put in is what it processes. What manifests in our world is a reflection of our thoughts.

A certain man started work with a network marketing company. He joyously reached out to his associates because he wanted them to join him. In his effort to convince them, he got shocked with their responses. Rather than getting them to join, his associates gave him one hundred and one reasons he would not succeed in his new business. The man felt disappointed and sober, but not put off. He refused to be defeated. He was of the opinion that whatever that has disadvantages must have advantages so he sorts them. He chose to remove the prefix *"dis"* from the said disadvantages his associates listed. He decided to see the brighter side of reasons not to succeed. Because he believed in himself, because he firstly convinced himself, he was able to turn the one hundred and one reasons not to succeed in his new business to one hundred and one reasons to succeed. Today he is among the successful people in the business, just because he believed he could.

CHAPTER THREE
FOCUS

"Lack of direction, not lack of time, is the problem. We all have twenty-four hour days"
– Zig Ziglar.

Have you ever been busy all day only to wonder what you accomplished at the end of the day? Distractions are time dumpsters disguised as productive pals. Most times, you see people mistake motion for action. You can actually be busy doing absolutely nothing. According to Steve Jobs, *"simple can be harder than complex; you have to work hard to get your thinking clean, to make it simple. But it is worth it at the end because once you get there, you can move mountains"* That is to say focus does the magic, mental toughness it is!

There is a saying I love so much: Jack-Of-All-Trades, master of none. Take for instance, you set of out to learn three languages. You make your arrangements, which include getting teacher(s). If you take the lectures simultaneously, that is learning all languages at the same time or even learning one language a today, language B tomorrow and languages C the day after tomorrow, chances are that you will not master any of the three languages. The ideal thing to do is to focus! I believe and it is foolproof that if you concentrate on learning one language at a time, you will save time and learning will be easier.

Self-development secret lies solely on concentration. When you focus intensely within yourself, you will discover and unlock your potentials. When you focus, you do not dissipate energies on irrelevant thoughts or activities, rather you conserve it! If you focus, you will be efficient and ultimately, take charge of your life. The skill of concentration is very vital in every kind of success, for without it no matter your effort, it would only amount to *"busy doing nothing"*. If you want to accomplish great things, you must master the art of focusing and concentrating.

The mind processes tasks before they manifest. What this means is that, when your mind is clear enough, it is easier to focus intensely on a task, hence solutions come quicker than when you occupy your mind with irrelevant thoughts.

If people must count on you for anything, you must possess a certain degree of self-confidence and that, can only come from a focused mind! If you must improve and become a sellable brand, there must be this level of concentration and focus in what you do. The more energy you put into who you are, the brighter and better you become.

When I was younger, I amazed at how a magnifying glass could ignite a piece of paper when rays of sun pass through it at one point. The 'magic' is that for the piece of paper to burn, the rays of sun must concentrate on a particular point through the magnifying glass for a given time. If you place the magnifying glass too close or farther away from the paper, nothing will happen to the paper.

This experiment explains how powerful concentration could be. Focusing is a skill that enables you to fix your attention on the goal you want to achieve while at the same time it excludes you from the awareness of every other thing happening around you.

CHAPTER FOUR

COMPASSION

"Compassion brings us to a stop, and for a moment we rise above ourselves"
– Mason Cooley

When we help and care for people, even if it does not benefit us we are simply being compassionate. Compassion is about expressing one's highest self ultimately.

When I took my father to the hospital for a medical check-up, I had the privilege to discuss with one of the medical practitioners at the hospital. In our many discourses, the doctor mentioned a 19-year-old female patient who was on the verge of losing a leg because she had no one to pay her bill for treatment. According to the doctor, the leg is infected and could be fatal. Treatment was possible, and she could walk on her feet if funds were available. I did not have the money needed for her treatment but I felt the need to do something. Therefore, I reached out to friends, family, and associates and within a short period, we raised more than what was required for her treatment. Today, she is back on her feet.

Being compassionate will not only endear you to people, it will also increase your confidence. You do not need to be stupendously rich to be compassionate; it is a thing of the heart. At any point, you should be willing to show kindness, care, and help others grow.

As a brand, if people notice that you are compassionate about them, I must say you are SOLD OUT! Clients will help advertise you; consequently, your network and your net worth will increase. "We learn to do by doing" what does this signify? Do not talk compassion; it is a way of life. Compassion is lived; do not say it, act it!

Here is a short story about compassion:

Jorge Munoz, a school bus driver had a tradition he maintained for years. He is a bus driver by day and an angel by night. Every night he goes home to cook food on his old stove. He then goes to street corner in Queens, New York and feed those that are hungry. He does this with his own money, the little he earns from his job. He is a man with a large heart, a man that always wants to help. This is the epitome of an everyday hero.

For me, compassion means giving people around you a treat as you would yourself. It does not matter whether they are family, friends, or total strangers.

What act of compassion have you done all your life? Like Mr. Munoz, you too can be an angel to people around you. You could actually leave smiles in people's faces.

If you want to prosper in what you do, be compassionate!

CHAPTER FIVE

ATTITUDE

"There is NOTHING either good or bad but THINKING makes it so!"

Attitude is a predisposition or tendency to respond positively or negatively towards certain objects, ideas, persons, or situations. Your attitude influences how you respond to challenges and your day-to-day choice of action. As a person who is success driven, you must let your state of mind reflect only positivity in all your dealings. Attitude distinguishes failure from success.

Let me tell you a story of two sales persons who went on a field trip to market for a shoe company. These fellows were tested marketers per excellence but they have different attitudes. Their employer was extremely confident of their ability to represent the company and sell their products. When the marketers got to their destination, they found that the people they have come to meet do not wear shoes. Attitude played out instantly. The marketers immediately put calls back to base. While Mr. A reported that there is a snag – that the people would not need their products because they do not use them, Mr. B saw an opportunity, and asked that more shoes be sent down, as people walked bare footed, more people would need shoes.

The scenario above paints a perfect picture of how attitude works. Life in general is 10% what happens to you and 90% how you react to it. You do not have to see difficulties when opportunity calls. Rather you are supposed to see opportunity in every difficulty!

As the most essential brand, your reaction to any situation matters. Your followers would love their leader to be one who is solution-oriented.

Have you wondered why two preachers would pick up the same portion of the scripture; while the audience of one may yearn for more, the audience of another would be fast asleep within a few minutes? It is all about how they see and react to things.

You cannot hide attitude. If you must win people's heart in your day to today activities, you must be charismatic. You must wear positivity like a cloak because whatever happens to you as a person is the resultant effect of your mind-set! You alone have the authority to give any situation in and around you a meaning.

Your interpretation of any given situation may differ from the person next to you. Therefore, strive to see opportunities where others see challenges; see solutions where others see problems. Do not feel discouraged because of naysayers; let your attitude differ from theirs. Your life will change for the best if you work on your attitude, if you condition your mind to see good in every bad situation. Be resolute, your attitude can make or mar you.

CHAPTER SIX
CONFIDENCE

"You either walk inside your story and own it or you stand outside your story and hustle" – Brene Brown.

You are capable of so much more than you realise. When you release your grasp on the physical structure (*comfort zone*) that holds you back, then, you will understand how far you can fly under your own power.

Within the world of our individual lives, we rely on our jobs, our spouses, our businesses – on many so-called structures. While sometimes we do need all these, we can also learn as we grow that these sources of safety do not always last. That which is lasting and permanent lies within us. It is our positive self-esteem and belief in our own unique abilities.

A business executive was deep in debt and could not see a way out. Creditors were closing in on him. Suppliers were demanding payment. He sat on the park bench, head in hands, and wondered if anything could save his company from bankruptcy, when suddenly an old man appeared before him and said, *"I can see that something is troubling you"*. After the business executive narrated his story, the old man retorted, *"I believe I can help you"*.

He asked the business executive his

name, wrote out a check, and pushed it into his hand saying, *"Take this money, meet me here exactly one year from today, and you can pay me back at that time"*. Then he turned and disappeared as quickly as he had come. The business executive saw in his hand a check for $500,000 signed by John D. Rockefeller, then one of the richest men in the world.

"I can erase my money worries in an instant," he realised. Instead, the executive decided to put the uncashed check in his safe. Just knowing it was there might give him the strength to work out a way to save his business, he thought.

With renewed optimism, he negotiated

better deals and extended terms of payment. He closed several big sales. Within few months, he was out of debt. Exactly one year later, he returned to the park with the uncashed check. At the agreed time, the old man appeared, but as the executive was about to hand back the check and share his success story, a nurse came running.

"I'm so glad I caught him," she cried. *"I hope he hasn't been bothering you. He's always escaping from the rest home and telling people he's John D. Rockefeller"*.

And she led the old man away by the arm; the astonished executive stood there stunned, all year long he had been wheeling and dealing, buying and selling, convinced he had half a million dollars behind him. Suddenly, the business executive realised that it was not the money, real or imagined that had turned his life around. His newfound self-confidence gave him the power to achieve anything he went after.

CHAPTER SEVEN

CREATIVITY

"The desire to create is one of the deepest yearnings of the human soul."
– Dieter F. Uchtdorf

You do not need to beat others to achieve your goals. If you have a task to undertake, your sole aim should be to accomplish.

Do not mistake creativity for intelligence, for they are by no means equivalent. A person can be intelligent but not creative. Creativity is adaptive, original, and realisable. Make creativity your way of life. Do not consign it to a brief episode.

Let me share with you an experience that

has helped shape me. I volunteered to partake in an experiment at a business meeting. The presenter at the event grouped the volunteers into five cells, comprising of four members – male and female alike. We were to perform a-four-minute assignment with a plastic straw, two sheets of paper, a fresh egg and a paper tape. To be successful in the task, you have to protect a fresh egg with the listed materials from breaking when released from a 6ft on the floor. I was the eldest and one with the highest educational qualification in my cell but I had absolutely no idea where to begin. Even with the grace of one added minute, my teammates and I could not finish. Two out of the five cells completed their assignment successfully.

After the business meeting, I walked up to one of the leaders of the group who were successful in the task to ask how they did it. I learnt that they did not rush to start like in my own group. They rather took a minute to nominate a leader, another minute to exchange ideas, and in the next minute, they completed the task. They got creative!

You can see that my educational qualification and level of intelligence could not protect the egg in my group. We have now established that there is no correlation between being intelligent and creative.

To become the most essential brand, you

have to distinguish yourself from the rest. Be the best you can, and to be that, you need creative abilities.

Creativity is more of mode of thinking than amount of intelligence. However, you will need a certain amount of intelligence to be creative. Whoever you are, wherever you are, you can improve your creative thinking by training. Although we can barely alter genetic factors, we can alter our behaviour through manipulations of our immediate environment. Culture, family, and education play big roles in the development of your creative thinking.

Creativity is contagious! If you want to be creative, you must check your circle of relations. Be in the circle of creative people, that way you are sure to develop your abilities. Creativity takes courage. Lose the fear of being wrong. Robert Bresson says, *"Make visible what, without you, might perhaps never have been seen"*.

CHAPTER EIGHT
PURPOSE

"If you hang out with chickens, you are going to cluck, and if you hang out with eagles, you are going to fly."
– Steve Maraboli

The moment you pause and ask *'Who am I?' 'Why am I here?' 'Why do I exist?'* Your journey to success has begun.

It is not in the nature of sane and successful people to leave their abode without a "Why". Your *Why*, is the most important aspect of your developmental processes.

As one who is determined to succeed,

you must discover your mission and envision it. Only then will your direction be clear enough for your journey.

You can start by asking yourself some of these questions:

- ➢ What is most important to me?
- ➢ What are my deepest values and beliefs?
- ➢ What are my concerns?

Take time to go through these questions. Notice what touches and inspires you about these questions. Write down your honest thoughts and answers that come to you as you ponder. Use what you have written as basis to design your life. You are the SOLE architect of your life!

There is a story of two young people

who had the opportunity to meet and greet a famous king. One was excited, but the other was not. When asked about the difference in their feelings, the excited one said, *"I have dreamt of meeting a king all my life. I want to know how powerful and magnificent it is like to be one,"* and the other just did not want to go. When asked why, he said *"Nothing"*.

From the story, it is evident that both of them have different views. While one was prepared to take advantage of the opportunity because he knows and understands his "why," the other was not prepared and at the same time does not know the reason why he does not want to go.

There are people like the second person in the world today. However, human beings have the ability to make choices. Your "why" is a guardian chip that controls your choices.

Success comes when you consistently persevere towards achieving your set goal. It means that there is a why (*purpose*) and that "why" propels you. The essence of knowing your why in any venture is to maintain discipline. Your why gives you reasons to stay focused.

I once met a woman who deals on used cans in Lagos, Nigeria. She treks the length and breadth of the city to pick these cans. Each time I saw this woman, I wondered why she snoops the streets and gutters for used cans, until I summoned courage to ask her. Her response was *"My son, I have two children. I want them to be well educated,"* there and then, I understood why she was taking such pain. She knows her "why," and it keeps her going. She does not mind how long it will take her to achieve her dream. People like her become successful.

What is your purpose now? Who are your associates? Does your purpose align with your associates? If your purpose differs from the people you spend time with, chances are that you will never realise them.

Being successful is directly proportional

to leading a purposeful life. In all you do or intend to do, always know your "why" beforehand. If you do not define your purpose, your venture will be useless. Always remember that the responsibility of your life and your limitations begins with you. Let your life be a purpose driven!

CHAPTER NINE
COMMITMENT

"Unless commitment is made, there are only promises and hopes… but no plans."

– Peter Druker

If you resolve to carry out a particular activity at a specified time, under a certain circumstance, and you realise it, you are committed.

Commitment is all about keeping your word. You as the most essential brand, must be willing to commit to people you deal with on daily basis. Commitment is not a description of your good looks or expensive outfits; it is a description of your character. To some extent, commitment is your mission. It is about the way you create and deliver your values. Commitment is that immense feeling you convey to your followers and people you deal with. What keeps or sacks you in business is your ability to keep to your promises, to deliver the exact values you promise. If you want to succeed, you must be willing to go all out to keep to your promises. Your word must be your bond!

In one of my vacations, I sought for a ticket to a massively publicised comedy show. I was about to part with some money for the ticket, when a woman made a negative remark about the event. In her words, *"Sir do not let them fool you, forget about the commercials. These people are fake! I spent my time and money to attend their show last year only to realise that the A-list artistes and comedians they advertised were not part of the event. I was totally disappointed"*. My desire for the show died instantly. All efforts by the ticket vendor to make me understand why the previous edition could not live up to its billing only amounted to damage control. Like me, others will not make it to the event because the organizers were not committed to their promises in the past.

It is better to promise less and deliver more! Do not say it if you will not do it. While building your brand, it is important to create and maintain confidence, content, and value that will distinguish you. If for instance you own a bakery, and have your customers believe you will sell to them fruit bread of a certain grams and at a certain amount, you have set a standard. For you to keep your customer base, you must be committed to it. If for any reason you need to change a thing, let your customers know.

Zig Ziglar posits, *"Most people who fail in their dream fail not from lack of ability but from lack of commitment."*

Uncommon results require uncommon commitment. There is no two ways about commitment; you are all in or nothing. There is no in-between. Do not paint a picture of you in a manner you would not be able to wear same long term. Let your inner self describe you to the people you deal with.

Reaching your lifetime goal requires 100% commitment. Just like an aircraft that needs its engines to be working at 100%, not even 99.9%; to succeed in life, you must be true to yourself and people around you!

CHAPTER TEN
STRENGTH/WEAKNESS

"An arch consists of two weakness which leaning on each other become a strength"
– Leonardo Da Vinci.

As the most essential brand, you must exhibit strengths and weaknesses. Exhibiting these traits is not in any way a flaw but it is being complete. Building your team in this manner surely will give you and your team best results.

According to Mother Theresa, *"you can do what I cannot do, I can do what you cannot do, and together we can do great things"*.

Apparently, one cannot be tall and short at the same time; in you lies a unique ability. Discovering your abilities and putting it to use would be one of your greatest achievements.

Let us digest and learn from a story of the turtle and the rabbit.

Once upon a time, a turtle and a rabbit had an argument about who was faster, so they decided to settle the argument with a race. The turtle and the rabbit both agreed on a route and started the race. The rabbit shot ahead and ran briskly for some time; then seeing that he was far ahead of the turtle, he decided to sit under a tree for some time and relax before continuing the race. He sat under the tree and soon fell asleep. The turtle plodding on overtook the rabbit and soon finished the race, and emerged the winner. The rabbit woke up and realised that it had lost the race. It felt disappointed that it lost the race because it had been overconfident, careless, and lax.

If the rabbit had not taken things for granted, there is no way the turtle could have won. Therefore, it challenged the turtle to another race. The turtle agreed. This time the rabbit went all out and ran without stopping from start to finish, it won by several miles. After the race, the turtle did some thinking and realised that there is no way he can beat the rabbit in a race. It thought for a while and challenged the rabbit to another race, but on a slightly different route. The rabbit agreed and they took off. In keeping to his self – made commitment to be consistently fast, the rabbit ran at top speed until it came to a broad river. The finish line was a couple of miles on the other side of the river, the rabbit sat there wondering what to do. In the meantime, the turtle trundled along. Got to the river, swam to the opposite bank, continued walking, and finished the race.

The turtle and the rabbit became good friends and they did some thinking together. They both realised that they could have been better at the last race if they ran as a team. Therefore, they decided to do the last race again, but to run as a team this time. The beginning of the race saw the rabbit carry the turtle on its back until they reached the riverbank, then the turtle took over and swam across with the rabbit on his back. At the other side of the river, the rabbit again carried the turtle and they reached the finish line together. Both the turtle and rabbit felt a greater sense of satisfaction than they had felt earlier.

From the story, it is evident that when you build your team around your strengths and weaknesses, they work to your advantage. You will enjoy huge successes if you harness and put to use your brilliance and competencies. Teamwork is mainly about situational leadership and letting the person with the relevant core competency for a particular situation take leadership. This way everybody wins.

CHAPTER ELEVEN

HEALTH

"Take care of your body, it's the only place you have to live" – Jim Rohn

The English Dictionary describes health as the state of being free from illness or injury. As the most essential brand, you must be in your best possible condition of health – physically and mentally – to be sellable.

According to Tom Stoppard, a healthy attitude is contagious. One does not have to wait to catch it from others but be a carrier. Therefore, you have to invest more in your health than anything else because the greatest wealth you can have is good health.

You have to be healthy to be successful. Of course, 80% of success is SHOWING UP! You can only attend and participate in a business meeting because you are healthy. If you are not bedridden, you can execute deals. Being healthy is a way of life and not a trend.

Recently, I decided to allow myself to rest as much as I work, and I also plan to give myself more vacation and less work sooner than later.

While growing up, I knew a hardworking man. This man acquired properties and amassed huge wealth – he was largely successful per se. Unfortunately, he never found time for rest, exercise, or medical check-up. His definition of relaxation was to consume alcohol and beef. For him, health was secondary. Years rolled by, and he took ill. It was a terminal condition and he had to sell all the properties he had acquired in a bid to raise money to save his life. Sadly, all his efforts came to nought. He lost his life.

He may have averted such trouble if he had time for his health, if he gave his body priority as much as he gave his business.

As a brand, you ought to be attractive, and being attractive entails healthy living. What people whom you deal with see first is how you look. You must be physically healthy for any client to go closer to know what you have to offer. This means that your business begins with taking proper care of yourself. Always find time to rest, exercise your body, eat to live, and routinely go for medical check.

CHAPTER TWELVE
SELF CONTROL/WILL POWER

"Feelings are much like waves, we can't stop them from coming but we can choose which one to surf"

Self-control is your ability to regulate your emotions, thoughts, and behaviour in any situation. As the most essential brand, your success is hugely dependent on your ability to control yourself, your emotions, your behaviours, and the way you react to situations.

Let us assume you got news of an unforeseen circumstance, which has led to a massive loss of your investments. How will you react? Will you be rock solid, calm, clearheaded and optimistic or will you throw tantrums, put the blame on other people or act further on impulse with probably bad choices that would worsen the situation? Ancient wisdom has it that a person without self-control is like a house with its doors and windows knocked out.

You become prone to all forms of harm, once you lose your self-control. As a brand, harm here means losing influence, respect, and trust from people, especially those you lead. Self-control is a personal skill developed in every good leader. If you can manage your emotions and behaviours positively, then you can lead.

Daniel Goleman once said this about

leaders with self-control, *"Reasonable people – the ones who maintain control over their emotions are the people who can sustain safe, fair environments"*. If your capacity for self-control is zero, the flip side is not good. It will definitely affect your performance negatively.

On one of my visits to a public official, I met a young man who looked very frustrated. From what I gathered, the young man was there to seal a business deal with the public official but it never materialised. This young man had waited a long time for that opportunity and when it came, he took it. Nevertheless, the deal was off the table as soon as it came, when his host's daughter suddenly appeared in the garden where he was waiting to enjoy the evening breeze. The beauty of that woman caught the attention of the young man to the extent that he did not notice his host had spent some time beside him. His host was disappointed and left words for him through his assistant. According to the assistant, his boss the public official will have no business with a man who cannot concentrate on business the way he concentrates on a woman's buttocks.

That young man lost the opportunity because he deviated from his mission. He let his emotion get the best of him. He could have been more alert to the business that took him there but he chose to feed his perversion and emotions. Of course, the consequence was devastating.

Successful people have control over every of their thought and action. Self-control is one attribute that refines your ability to choose between success and failure. If you learn to control yourself, you can master absolutely everything!

CHAPTER THIRTEEN

BALANCE

"You can do anything, but not everything"

– David Allen

As life is about holding on and letting go, so is business. You cannot win all the time. In every bad situation, there are good. Every situation has its good and bad but your ability to strike a balance distinguishes you from the rest. As a brand you, you do not search for balance, you create it. Know where you are and where you want to be at a specified period. Every bitterness has some sweetness; what makes you unique is your ability to shift your paradigm and strike a balance.

Let me share a story that has repositioned me for the better. Perhaps it might be helpful to you too. It is a story of a DRUNKARD.

There lived a drunkard who no one took seriously. He was a person with no regard until he decided to change people's perception of him. One day, he had a deep thought about his person; he re-evaluated his life and found himself wanting. He was sober and needed to do something differently. He was determined to change his aura. Suddenly, he had an idea of what he needed to do. He went to see his king at his palace but the gatekeepers did not allow him entrance. The gatekeepers restrained him but he kept knocking until he got the king's attention. The king ordered him in. In the presence of the king, he said that his mission was for the king to allow him to walk on the river. Everyone, including the king laughed at his request. The king asked the drunkard to leave as he had other serious matters to attend. The king also asked him to go walk on the river if it is his wish, since he knew his way to it. The drunkard protested but the king excused himself.

That incident did not deter the drunkard. He went back to the palace several but the king did not grant him audience yet he persisted. The king grew tired of his constant disturbance but also admired his courage and persistence, so he ushered him in. The drunkard asked the king to grant him the opportunity to walk on the river. The king asked him to go and do so. The drunkard protested again but this time the king decided to hear him. The drunkard pleaded with the king to send word to everyone to assemble around the riverbank that people may watch him walk on the river. The king was awed. The king warned that there would be severe consequences if the drunkard did not walk on water upon assembling people in the community. The drunkard answered that he is ready to accept any punishment if he fails. The king approved his request. The drunkard had two weeks to prepare while the king sent out word to the community. In the event that the drunkard fails, he would face banishment from the community. The drunkard went home happy that day knowing the opportunity he sought to strike a balance in his life has come.

The day came, everyone, including the king gathered at the riverbank. The drunkard emerged from the crowd. Alas! He walked on water, to the admiration of everyone. There were applause, praises, and amazement.

The drunkard had achieved his goal!

People began to wonder how it happened. Some believed it was magic. Two people summoned courage to ask the drunkard how he did it. The drunkard asked them to meet him at the river at midnight if they were interested to know. They accepted and left. While they were leaving, one of them told the other that he would not go to the river by midnight, that he has confirmed his curiosity. To him, the drunkard walked on water only by magic. The other persisted, and at midnight, he went to meet the drunkard at the river. At the meeting, the drunkard told him that when the king gave him the opportunity to walk on water, he went there at midnight to put stones in his walk pace, and practiced until he mastered where the stones were. The drunkard also told the man that if he knew where the stones were, he too could walk on water.

You can always strike a balance in your

life and endeavours. Understand that no matter how far you have gone on a wrong lane, you can still make a turn-around and go the right lane.

Life is to every one of us the meaning we give to it!

CHAPTER FOURTEEN
FINANCIAL FREEDOM

"One is ONLY poor if they choose to be"

– Dolly Parton

Financial freedom is a state of having sufficient wealth to live without having to work actively for necessities. In other words, people can actually become financially free if they have the ability to sustain their chosen lifestyle without ever having to work again.

As the most essential brand, you must be financially intelligent to become financially free.

I will take you on practical steps to achieve financial freedom. What you make of these steps and the rate at which you can move from where you currently are to your desired destination lies solely within you. It is very possible to attain financial freedom. You can achieve it if you make it a goal to follow these steps.

Currently, there are about five types of passive incomes namely: Real Estate, Paper Investment, Intellectual Property, Network Marketing, and Automated Business.

You can generate passive income only from business or investor quadrants and not from the employee or self-employed quadrant. Let us take it one after another.

Real Estate:

Real Estate, originally known as Royal

Estate (*meant for kings then*) is an income generating means that will always be significant. It is one of the most secured and long lasting of all known forms of passive income. You can earn good money from real estate business. Income generated from this wheel of income is known as *"rental income"*. Most people are scared and often times believe that they do not have the capability and or opportunity to get involved in real estate because it requires huge capital. However, you can become a player in real estate business by accumulating money in your escrow account until you are able to take a chance in the business. When investing in real estate, experts advice that you invest for rental in the stead of appreciation. Rental will always give you cash flow. In other words, it is wise to build to rent other than build to live. I know of a landlord who lives as a tenant few poles from his property (house); people might think he is a fool, but that is being FINANCIAL INTELLIGENT. Play at the bottom of the pyramid then grow upwards.

Paper Investment:

Paper Investments are investments where what you have for keeps are certificates stating details of such investments. In this category, we have businesses like stocks, bonds, treasury bills, fixed deposits, etc. Incomes made from PAPER INVESTMENTS (*PI*) are dividends return on investment (*ROI*) or interest.

Huge amounts of money is required if you are to have a meaningful investment that can give you meaningful passive income. This however, must not deter you. Starting small is not a bad idea, as you can build huge asset from the little you have now.

This type of investment is a good one but because of inconsistency in leveraging, it is advised that you invest with long term in mind; say between 5 - 20 years.

Automated Business:

I personally recommend this to you. Automated business gives you the freedom you need because most times you are not physically involved in the business. It gives you comfort, that is to say you have control over it.

Any business put together and can sustain itself, is an automated business. For instance, if you buy a franchise of an already established business, deal on online business or e-commerce, you are an automated businessperson.

Intellectual Property:

Intellectual is one of the greatest of all when it comes to income wheels. Intellectual property are creations of a person's mind for which he or she has personal rights according to law.

For instance, speaking, writing, movie acting, singing, software developing, innovations etc. are all intellectual properties. Royalty is what you earn from intellectual property. Everyone is unique and can venture into this kind of business.

Network Marketing:

Network marketing also known as multi-level marketing, is a type of marketing designed to reward participants for sales they attract directly, and for sales people they recruit into their team attract. You can do this type of marketing of either products or services by word of mouth or relationship referrals. Most people often confuse network-marketing business for pyramid or Ponzi scheme. There are various types of network marketing, which include but not limited to uni-level, binary, and hybrid. Of all the income wheels, I strongly advise you to go for network marketing business because its model suits the interactive and social nature of people. Many companies and industries are already using networking to grow their businesses.

Anyone can venture into this business, as its start-up capital is not too tasking yet the rewards are enormous.

If possible, you can participate actively in every of these steps to financial freedom. The more income streams you have, the better and faster you could become financially free. Keep increasing your earnings, manage your expenses properly, save, and then invest in assets that will increase your passive income sources. That way in few years, you will be FINANCIALLY FREE!

CHAPTER FIFTEEN

GIVING

"We rise by lifting others"

- Robert Ingersoll

According to Anne Frank, *"No one has ever become poor by giving"*. There are no poverty in our societies rather lack of will to GIVE. Therefore, if I give, you give, and everyone else gives, there would be no lack in our societies.

As the most essential brand, the fastest way to grow financially and otherwise is to embrace and practice the culture of giving. Take it upon yourself to be a source of happiness and inspiration to at least one or more persons a day.

Giving is not just about handing out cash to people: knowledge impartation, skill transfer etc. are some of the best gifts one can ever give.

In one of my road trips, the activity of a young man and his friends inspired me. While I pulled over to take a phone call, I watched in amazement these "angels" as they fed the less privilege persons begging along the road. Their action touched me so much that I decided to find out who they were. People around informed me that the young man and his friends feed those people twice every day. According to people, these young men have also succeeded in taking hundreds of people off the streets by way of education and skills acquisition.

Impressed by this act of humanity, I had to approach them to ask why they were doing what they are doing; their response was, "when we give, we receive in folds. The joy of seeing smiles on their faces keeps us going".

I understood that the young man started giving to the less privileged when he had little. Now he is rich because he chose to give. He is rich because people are happy. He is rich because people can smile, and he is rich because people can feed through him.

I learnt the lesson of my life after that encounter. The quantity you give does not matter, what matters is your willingness to give to humanity. If you want to grow, you have to give. Go out today and GIVE someone a gift that would change his or her life for the better!

www.ingramcontent.com/pod-product-compliance
Lightning Source LLC
Chambersburg PA
CBHW022122040426
42450CB00006B/800